Male Victims of Elder Abuse

Their Experiences and Needs

Jacki Pritchard

Jessica Kingsley Publishers
London and Philadelphia

First published in the United Kingdom in 2001 by
Jessica Kingsley Publishers Ltd,
116 Pentonville Road, London
N1 9JB, England
and
325 Chestnut Street,
Philadelphia PA 19106, USA.

www.jkp.com

Library of Congress Cataloging in Publication Data
A CIP catalog record for this book is available from the Library of Congress

British Library Cataloguing in Publication Data
A CIP catalogue record for this book is available from the British Library

ISBN 1 85302 999 8

Printed and Bound in Great Britain by
Athenaeum Press, Gateshead, Tyne and Wear

Male Victims of Elder Abuse

Violence and Abuse Series

This new series forms a set of accessible books for practitioners, managers and policy makers working in social and health care, probation and criminology. Each book draws on a key piece of research or current practice relating to violence and abuse to give practical guidance on new ways of working with both victims and perpetrators to bring about positive change.

of related interest

Good Practice with Vulnerable Adults
Edited by Jacki Pritchard
ISBN 1 85302 892 3

Becoming a Trainer in Adult Abuse Work
A Practical Guide
Jacki Pritchard
ISBN 1 85302 913 0

Working with Elder Abuse
A Training Manual for Home Care, Residential and Day Care Staff
Jacki Pritchard
ISBN 1 85302 418 X

The Abuse of Older People
A Training Manual for Detection and Prevention, 2nd edition
Jacki Pritchard
Foreword by Eric Sainsbury
ISBN 1 85302 305 1

Narrative Approaches to Working with Adult
Male Survivors of Child Sexual Abuse
The Clients', the Counsellor's and the Researcher's Story
Kim Etherington
ISBN 1 85302 818 5

Geronticide
Killing the Elderly
Mike Brogden
ISBN 1 85302 709 X

Contents

Acknowledgements

It is important to thank the three social services departments who participated in the original project and the Joseph Rowntree Foundation for funding the research.

In addition, special thanks are due to the managers and workers within the day/resource centres, who were so supportive in helping me to work with male victims and give this important issue the recognition it deserves.

I am indebted to two people who supported me during the original project and through this current work. First, Eric Sainsbury, who once again has been invaluable in acting as my 'sounding board' and reading the drafts of this book. Second, Melanie Whitehouse, whose patience seems infinite when transcribing tapes from interview.

Finally, I am very grateful to all the men who have spoken so willingly to me in focus groups and in interview, because without their openness this important work could not have been undertaken.

Note

The Joseph Rowntree Foundation has supported this project as part of its programme of research and innovative development projects, which it hopes will be of value to policy makers and practitioners. The facts presented and views expressed in this book are, however, those of the author and not necessarily those of the Foundation.

Introduction

This book is about men who have been abused in later life: they are victims of elder abuse. Some of them have also been abused in childhood or earlier in adulthood. Indeed, some may be said to have suffered a lifetime of abuse. Before discussing the life experiences and needs of these male victims, it is necessary to consider elder abuse in more general terms, recognising that this a subject which to date has been largely ignored, but is an essential context to the more specific problems associated with male victims.

Elder abuse is not a new phenomenon; it has been around for centuries, though we have often failed to refer to it in such terms. Shakespeare was writing about two male victims of elder abuse when he wrote *King Lear*. The abuse of older people is certainly not something new for the twenty-first century yet it is not given the high profile which its incidence deserves. One of the reasons for this is that in some societies older people are not given much respect; they may be seen as an economic burden on society because they are no longer economically productive. In societies which emphasise youthful vigour, old age will tend to have a very negative image; consequently, younger people may come to fear growing old. Becoming frail, disabled or incapacitated are typical stereotypes of older people despite the reality that being old can bring new experiences and many new rewards. Another consequence of ageism is that if people do not want to think about the inevitability of old age, they may avoid interacting with old people and also avoid watching, listening or reading about the 'nasty things' which can happen to an older person. Thus, elder abuse is frequently swept under the carpet, both by professionals and by the public at large.

Not surprisingly, therefore, elder abuse does not get the same media attention as child abuse. The bottom line is that older people are not as acceptably emotive as children. Nevertheless, progress is being made in this important subject and it may be useful to the reader initially to discuss some of the key developments in recent years before turning attention to the plight of male victims.

Terminology and developments

In the 1970s and 1980s the terms 'granny-bashing' and 'granny-battering' were in general use. At that time no one was offended by the term but interestingly there was no mention of 'grandad-bashing'! Some professionals had started to acknowledge that older people were being mistreated or harmed. Two geriatricians working with older people highlighted the problem as early as 1975 (Baker 1975; Burston 1975, 1977), but there was little public or professional reaction to their work. The real pioneer in giving prominence to the problem was Mervyn Eastman, who was employed as a social worker with special responsibilities for older people. He used the term 'old age abuse' and defined it as:

> the systematic maltreatment, physical, emotional or financial, of an elderly person…this may take the form of physical assault, threatening behaviour, neglect and abandonment or sexual assault. (Eastman 1984, p.3)

Eastman's work focused very much on the theory of carer's stress in domestic settings. This ran parallel with research which was being undertaken in North America at the time.

As early as 1981, elder abuse had been referred to in the US Senate as 'a national epidemic' (quoted in Riley 1989 p. 1). In the UK, recognition of and progress towards addressing this social problem were slow. A major conference was convened by the British Geriatrics Society in 1988 to raise awareness about the problem and at that time a few social services departments had started to develop policies and procedures on elder abuse (Tomlin 1989). Kent Social Services Department was the first to produce guidance for practitioners and many authorities subsequently followed suit (Kent Social Services Department 1987). In the early 1990s there was some debate about whether 'mistreatment' was a more appropriate term than 'abuse' when considering how older people were harmed. Since then, the adoption of the term 'elder abuse' has been widespread. In 1992 the Social Services Inspectorate produced *Confronting Elder Abuse*, which presented findings of research which had been undertaken in two London boroughs (Department of Health 1992). As a result of that research, practice guidelines were produced in the following year entitled *No Longer Afraid: The Safeguard of Older People in Domestic Settings* (Department of Health 1993). The definition of elder abuse was set broadly enough to include neglect and sexual abuse, neither of which had been given much attention previously because of the assumption of their low incidence:

Abuse may be described as physical, sexual, psycho-
logical, or financial. It may be intentional or uninten-
tional, or the result of neglect. It causes harm to the
older person, either temporarily or over a period of
time. (Department of Health 1993, p.3)

It should be noted that the research studies which had been
undertaken previously were highlighting that all these
forms of abuse were prevalent and consequently warranted
attention as separate categories of abuse rather than being
included under the more generalised phrase of physical
abuse.

In the years that followed, organisations working with
other vulnerable adults (e.g. those with disabilities, mental
health problems) highlighted the need for multi-agency
working to address the abuse of *all* vulnerable adults and
many social care agencies began to develop policies using
the term 'adult abuse'. In March 2000, *No Secrets: Guidance
on Developing and Implementing Multi-Agency Policies and Procedures to Protect Vulnerable Adults from Abuse* was launched
by the Minister of Health, John Hutton, at a national conference organised jointly by Action On Elder Abuse, UK
Voice and the Ann Craft Trust. This document states that a
vulnerable adult is a person:

who is or may be in need of community care services
by reason of mental or other disability, age or illness;
and who is or maybe unable to take care of him or
herself, or unable to protect him or herself against significant harm or exploitation. (Department of Health
2000a, pp.8–9)

Abuse is defined as a 'violation of an individual's human and civil rights by any other person or persons' (Department of Health 2000a, p.9).

It would seem that at last the issue of adult abuse was being taken seriously. Unfortunately, intervention is still not regarded as a statutory duty in the public services, despite the moral imperatives implicit in these various statements. However, a circular issued from the Department of Health (2000b, p.2) states: 'Directors of Social Services will be expected to ensure that the local multi-agency codes of practice are developed and implemented by 31st October 2001'.

So the requirement is that all agencies who work with vulnerable adults will have to develop systems to help adults who are victims of abuse, though an ongoing problem will be the lack of adequate funding for the resources necessary to work with both victims and abusers in the long term, that is to ensure adequate and lasting resolutions to the problems rather than short-term crisis management of the sticking-plaster kind.

Research

Even though elder abuse has not had a high profile to date, small research studies have been undertaken. Obtaining funding for research into elder or adult abuse can be difficult and consequently there have been no large-scale research projects in the UK. Research has been limited and has hitherto focused on what constitutes elder abuse and definitions of abuse (McCreadie 1996). But in addition there has been some work on prevalence, incidence and the characteristics of cases; there has been some predictive work on who is likely to be a victim or abuser. Many more studies have been undertaken in North America, the findings of which have been used for developing professional awareness in the UK.

Significantly and, in my view, unfortunately, some earlier research has given prominence to the somewhat limited factor of carer's stress as a root cause of much elder abuse. Thus, certain stereotypes have developed which can have the effect of distorting the focus of professional help and the time allocated to providing it. For example:

> the majority [of victims] are female, over 80 and are dependent as a result of physical or mental incapacity. (Eastman 1984, p.41)

> The abuser is typically identified as being female, middle aged and usually the offspring of the abused. (Gelles and Cornell 1985, p.104)

It is important to acknowledge that, valuable though these studies were, later work has challenged the stereotypes to which they unintentionally gave rise. When research and knowledge is limited we can make errors and since the 1980s we have learnt a great deal and moved on. The main lesson of more recent studies has been that elder abuse is a complex issue; there can be a variety of causal factors and associations contributing to an abusive situation. It is certainly unwise to continue to follow one causation theory such as carer's stress. As Biggs, Phillipson and Kingston (1995) have said:

> In order to understand elder mistreatment it is necessary to have a framework that explains the phenome-

non at a number of levels. We would suggest that an adequate explanation should be able to take at least three levels into account:

1. the social and historical context of mistreatment, in other words, how it is socially constructed;

2. the interplay of social actors within that social space, or how key figures interact with each other;

3. the way that the problem is conceived by individuals involved, and how they respond psychologically. (Biggs *et al.* 1995, p.29)

Many theories could be put forward to explain why abuse happens: e.g. situational model, exchange theory, symbolic interactionist theory, social construction of old age and political economy (Biggs *et al.* 1995). It is necessary to have an understanding of the different theories and look at each elder abuse case individually.

As well as trying to explain why elder abuse happens, recent researchers have also undertaken quantitative studies in order to ascertain the prevalence and incidence of elder abuse. Statistics differ greatly depending on the definitions of abuse which are used. Over the years, there has been a consensus of opinion that probably between 5 and 10 per cent of older people suffer some form of abuse (Pritchard 1995). One must always remember, however, that research inevitably focuses on people who are known to agencies; there is likely to be a large number of people who never have contact with any agency and whose abuse may remain well hidden. Therefore, the real prevalence is probably much higher.

Bearing in mind the limitations of scope and funding for research in this area of human need and social policy, certain matters remain inadequately explored. I have drawn attention to some of these in an earlier publication:

> little attention has been given to the needs of victims and the services they may require in both the short and long term...There has been very little research into how to work with victims of elder abuse in the long term... In recent years there has been renewed emphasis on *policy* – its development and implementation – within social and health care agencies; but the outcome has been to provide procedural frameworks for identifying abuse and for carrying out formal investigations [rather than for enhancing the skills of intervention]. The present project set out to consider the *provision of services* to victims (from agencies in all sectors). In doing so, it moves the debate from policy and procedures to practices and professional competence. (Pritchard 2000, pp.9–10, emphases in original)

Key issues for the future

It is important to have policies and procedures in place to work effectively with elder abuse, but it is also crucial for researchers, policy-makers and practitioners to develop knowledge and understanding of why abuse happens and how both victims and abusers can be helped. It is crucial that we get away from thinking about the 'typical case' and from the risks of stereotyping the victim and abuser.

We need also to broaden our perspective; many important issues still need more attention. Three important examples are abuse by strangers, abuse in institutions, and neglect and self-neglect.

Abuse by strangers

Historically the emphasis has been on older people who are abused by people known to them (family, neighbours, friends). Many older people are targeted by strangers because they are vulnerable. Isolated older people may be befriended by a stranger and then financially abused. Gangs of children or teenagers may harass older people in the community (Pritchard 1993, 1995).

Abuse in institutions

It is only in recent years that systematic attention has been given to the existence of abuse in institutions, even though it has been anecdotally acknowledged that maltreatments have always gone on in hospitals and residential homes (Clough 1988; Wagner Committee 1988) and that institutions can sometimes develop aberrant practices.

Neglect and self-neglect

Neglect as a form of abuse has gained more recognition since the late 1980s but very rarely in the UK is self-neglect (as a secondary consequence) included in definitions of abuse. Yet self-neglect is an issue which receives frequent comment from practitioners; many now wonder whether abuse procedures are appropriate and should be implemented when it is identified. There are important issues of causation and choice here which, in my view, are a great deal more complicated than is usually recognised in the hurly-burly of day-to-day welfare practice.

These three key issues are all relevant to the abuse of older men, which is the subject of this book. For years it has been assumed that it is mainly women who are subjected to abuse; men have been largely ignored. When I worked as a social worker, I came across a number of older men who were abused; in subsequent research projects men have been identified as victims of abuse (Pritchard 1995). In my most recent research project, which focused on women, I found that some men voluntarily came forward and identified themselves as victims. Given that, in our culture, it is far from easy for men to acknowledge weakness and dependency, these voluntary admissions of abuse came as something of a surprise. It was almost as if a social taboo was being broken. Clearly the subject invited further study.

This book has been written in order to give attention to the problems of older men in abusive situations. It focuses on their experiences and needs, and it gives them a voice so that professional workers and other helpers can develop a better understanding of the help for which they are asking.

CHAPTER 1

Men
Victims of Abuse

When one thinks about a victim of abuse an image of a child or woman usually springs into mind. Although it is wrong to stereotype we all do it; it is a fact of life conditioned from birth. During the 1980s and 1990s awareness has been raised about the prevalence of both child abuse and domestic violence, which has reinforced the images of stereotypical victims of abuse – children and women. Very little has been written about men as victims. When this has been addressed it has been in relation to male survivors of child sexual abuse (Etherington 1995; Hunter 1990; Mendel 1995) or to the male as a victim of domestic or spouse abuse (Gelles and Straus 1988; Steinmetz 1978; Straus and Gelles 1986; Straus, Gelles and Steinmetz 1980). This approach is too narrow and restrictive. It is necessary to look at the male victim of abuse in a wider context rather than confining research and analysis to previous definitions in terms of child abuse and domestic violence.

It has to be acknowledged (and accepted) that a male of any age can be abused. There may be resistance to this for a variety of reasons. For example, it is often hard to imagine that a man who is physically larger than a woman could be abused. Cultural norms and beliefs hold that women are much less violent than men. Furthermore, a man is usually assumed to be able to hold his own among members of his own sex, choosing to enter or avoid situations which will demonstrate his strength or weakness; in other words, men are not expected, individually, to be pushed around by others. Nevertheless, there is evidence to show that men are abused and the task of this book is to provide illustrative material about the kinds of abuse experienced by a group of older men and how they felt about their personal and social circumstances. Particular attention will be given to the extent and relevance of services' responsiveness to their needs.

First, however, we need briefly to consider some relevant information from research within the fields of child abuse and domestic violence. Many of the debates which have taken place in the 1970s, 1980s and 1990s have been about prevalence and incidence. In studies regarding child sexual abuse, estimates of prevalence vary enormously, because of differences in the definition of abuse, the populations surveyed, and whether statistical evidence is based on reports from agencies or self-report. Researchers have also focused on comparisons between the numbers of male and female child victims.

Similarly, when domestic violence has been researched, there have been heated debates about the comparative number of wives and husbands who have been abused, but also about the level and types of violence inflicted. Gelles (1997) commented:

It is quite clear that men are struck by their wives. It is also clear that because men are typically larger than their wives and usually have more social resources at their command, that they do not have as much physical or social damage inflicted on them as is inflicted on women. (Gelles 1997, p.93)

Steinmetz (1978) argued, however, that husband abuse was the most under-reported form of family violence and that women could in fact be more violent that men. During the 1970s and 1980s there was much debate about the analysis of the various research studies. But the issue of male victims has never really been pursued in the same way as other aspects of family and domestic violence:

Violence by wives has not been an object of public concern....In fact, our 1975 study was criticised for presenting statistics on violence by wives. (Straus and Gelles 1986, p.465)

What is important is the fact that men *are* abused, and it is sad to consider that maybe this area of research has not been pursued because in the past people have used or ignored research evidence for political wrangling, particularly in support of fashionable ideologies:

Despite all the evidence about female-on-male violence, many groups actively try to suppress coverage of the issue. Steinmetz received verbal threats and anonymous phone calls from radical women's groups threatening to harm her children after she published 'The Battered Husband Syndrome' in 1978. (*Washington Post*, 28th December 1993)

Mr Straus said at least 30 studies of domestic violence – including some he's conducted – have shown both sexes to be equally culpable. But he said some of the research, such as a recent Canadian national survey 'left out data on women abusing men...because it's politically embarrassing'....Women and men 'are almost identical' in terms of the frequency of attacks such as slapping, shoving, kicking. (*Washington Times*, 31st January 1994)

Straus (1999) has written about how the 'vitriolic controversy' had subsided by 1997. He says that one reason for this is 'the overwhelming accumulation of evidence from more than a hundred studies showing approximate equal assault rates' (Straus 1999, p.18).

Most of the debates which have spanned twenty years have taken place in North America. However, in 1996, the British Home Office published research which showed that men are just as likely as women to be victims of domestic violence. 4.2 per cent of men and the same percentage of women said they were assaulted each year (Home Office 1996).

There is some evidence, therefore, that men are abused both in childhood and in adult marriages or cohabitations. Research has focused predominantly on defining the abuse of males in physical and sexual terms. In line with my earlier work, I intend to broaden the focus of inquiry to include other forms of abuse (financial, neglect and emotional abuse). This is an area of research which has been totally neglected to date, probably because males are mostly seen in the role of perpetrator.

Attention to older men (whether married or single) as victims of abuse has been limited. In elder abuse studies statistics are usually presented regarding gender, with arguments focusing on the fact that more females than males are abused. Such studies are important and it is not my intention to minimise them. However, no matter how many males are abused compared to females, purchasers and providers of services have a responsibility to give consideration to the needs of these men. As a man grows older, he may become more vulnerable which in turn can make him more at risk of physical or emotional harm. Qualitative research can help to identify the needs of abused men and this is the subject of this book.

The purpose in writing this book

This book will consider the male as a victim of elder abuse. It will show two dimensions indicating similarities with the findings of earlier work on female victims (Pritchard 2000): first, that males may suffer the same types of abuse as females (though the proportions of the types may differ); and second, that males may experience similar patterns of abuse within their lifetimes, i.e. that an individual male may have experienced recurrent abusive situations during his life. The implications will also be apparent that although elder abuse should not be seen in isolation from the findings of studies within other age-groups, there are ways in which it needs to be considered and defined in its own terms rather than a subsidiary or secondary to more fashionable concerns in social policy and social care.

The purpose of this book is to present the findings of the project in regard to older men, that is, to discuss their experiences of abuse and their current needs. Abuse of men will be considered in terms of physical, emotional, financial, neglect and sexual experiences, and will include abuse by strangers as well as by intimates.

Background to the research project

This current book has resulted from a research project entitled *The Needs of Older Women: Services for Victims of Elder Abuse and Other Abuse* (Pritchard 2000), which was carried out between 1997 and 1999 in three social services departments located in the North of England:

- Churchtown
- Millfield
- Tallyborough.

While the original project was being undertaken, a considerable number of men were identified as being victims of elder abuse through the monitoring systems which had been set up. Furthermore, some men also asked to be involved in the project (this will be discussed in detail below). Consequently, the focus of inquiry broadened to include men but these findings were not included in the report on women. It was felt that they had a significance which merited separate attention.

As the present book grew out of the work of an earlier project, it will be helpful to the reader to summarise the project's main aims, which were to:

1. identify women who were victims of elder abuse

2. carry out a small study to identify the extent to which victims of elder abuse have also experienced abuse earlier in their lives

3. identify the types of abuse experienced (in childhood and adulthood)

4. identify the needs of victims

5. consider what resources or services should be provided for victims.

Methodology

The methods adopted for the research project needed to fulfil two main objectives:

1. to collect quantitative data regarding the victims, abusers and types of abuse

2. to collect qualitative data about victims' experiences of abuse and to identify need, *both* for protection *and* in coming to terms with their abusive experiences.

A full explanation of the methods used may be found in the original research report (Pritchard 2000). Data regarding male victims were collected by the use of

- monitoring forms and questionnaires

- focus groups and talks

- in-depth interviews with male victims

- telephone interviews with workers

- case files, case conferences minutes and protection plans.

Definition of elder abuse

Many definitions of elder abuse exist and can be open to interpretation. For the purposes of the research project, the following definition was adopted:

> Abuse may be described as physical, sexual, psychological or financial. It may be intentional or unintentional or the result of neglect. It causes harm to the older person, either temporarily or over a period of time. (Department of Health 1993, p.3)

This definition was used in conjunction with the adult abuse policies and procedures already established in Churchtown and Millfield and a working document which existed in Tallyborough.

How the male victims were identified

Systems were set up in all three departments in order to carry out a small quantitative study regarding adult abuse and also to identify possible female victims for interview within a qualitative study. It was while focus groups were being run in day centres and resource centres that some older men asked to participate in the project. Initially they wanted to attend the focus groups. When this began to occur on a regular basis, it was decided that the focus of inquiry should broaden to include men. Focus groups were run for over 300 older people attending day care facilities not only in order to identify women for in-depth interviews, but also to gain data from a large number of women. Users of the facilities became very well aware of what the researcher was undertaking and it was at this point that men came forward to participate in the groups. They were allowed to do so after this had been discussed with and agreed by the women. Men were also subsequently referred to the project via the managers of day care and respite facilities.

Consequently, men were allowed to attend the focus groups (with the permission of the women in the groups) and in-depth interviews were carried out with twelve men who had been victims of elder abuse. Thus, the numbers on which this report is based is small and, in part, self-selected. The information provided does, however, indicate the scope of experiences and needs with which professional helpers need to be concerned.

CHAPTER 2

Quantitative Findings

In the research project, statistics were compiled from monitoring forms during an 18-month period. Across the three departments 186 cases were cited where vulnerable adults were victims of abuse. Of these, 126 were older people (aged 60+), 29 of whom were older men. After the project had been formally concluded, the researcher continued to collect data and to analyse the monitoring forms in two departments, Churchtown and Tallyborough. For the following 12-month period 71 additional vulnerable adult cases were cited; there were 72 victims because one case involved a married couple. The statistical findings were very similar to the previous monitoring period; that is, the largest service group (66 per cent) of victims of adult abuse were older people.

It is not the purpose of this book to repeat the original findings concerning women (Pritchard 2000). Overall, the number of male victims of abuse, both younger and older, was sufficient to support the belief that it is wrong to think of females as the only victims. It will be helpful to present some of the main statistical findings, in which the statistics for the original project and for the following year have been combined.

Vulnerable adults

In the two periods of monitoring, a total of 258 vulnerable adults were identified as victims of abuse. Table 2.1 and Figure 2.1 illustrate the breakdown between the departments.

Table 2.1 Vulnerable adults	
Department	*Number*
Churchtown	115
Millfield	70
Tallyborough	73
Total	258

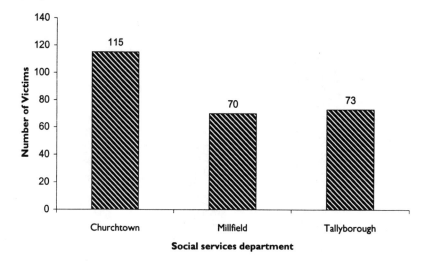

Figure 2.1 Adult abuse victims

Older people

The project identified an older person as any adult over 60 years of age; 171 older people were identified as victims of abuse, which constituted 66 per cent of the total number of vulnerable adults (see Table 2.2 and Figure 2.2).

Table 2.2 Number of older people identified as vulnerable adults	
Department	*Number*
Churchtown	82
Millfield	42
Tallyborough	47
Total	171

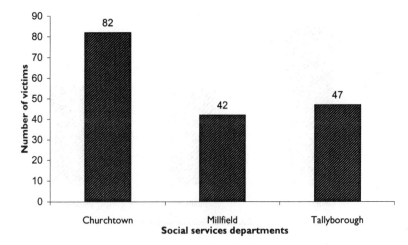

Figure 2.2 Victims of elder abuse

Gender

Over the years research studies have found more females than males to be victims of elder abuse (McCreadie 1996). This project similarly found that there were more female victims than male. However, a significant number of abused men were identified and this should not be overlooked. Over one-fifth (23 per cent) of older victims were male (see Table 2.3 and Figure 2.3).

Table 2.3 Gender of elder abuse victims		
	Female	*Male*
Churchtown	68	14
Millfield	30	12
Tallyborough	34	13
Total	132	39

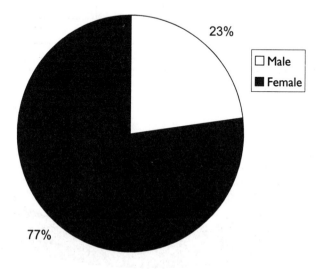

Figure 2.3 Gender of elder abuse victims

Age

Within the total number of abused older people, the majority were aged over 75 years old (58 per cent), which supports previous findings that more 'older elderly' are victims of abuse. Table 2.4 and Figure 2.4 show the ages of older victims, which ranged from 60 years to 99 years.

Table 2.4 Ages of older victims		
Age	*All victims*	*Male victims*
60–64	12	4
65–69	14	6
70–74	21	6
75–79	21	4
80–84	27	5
85–89	33	6
90–94	18	1
95–99	1	0
NK*	24	7
Total	171	39

Note: NK = not known

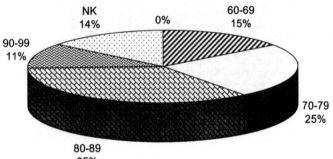

Figure 2.4 Ages of older victims

It will be noted, when considering male victims, that there was more equality across the age ranges and an equal divide between those abused under and over the age of 75 years (see Figure 2.5).

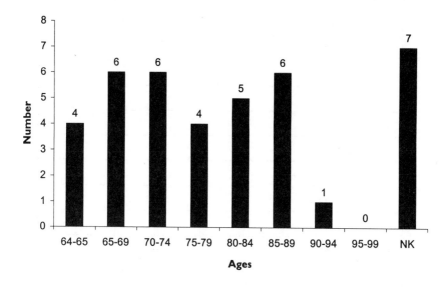

Figure 2.5 Ages of male victims

Physical or medical conditions

It has been argued that the older elderly are at risk of being abused because their physical and/or mental dependence may cause stress for their carers. I have argued elsewhere that this is far too simplistic (Pritchard 1995, 2000). Yet physical and mental health are important factors as they can make an older person vulnerable and an easy target for abuse. The majority of male victims had the range of

problems as shown in Table 2.5, which caused social
workers to describe their condition on monitoring forms
as 'frail and elderly'.

Table 2.5 Physical, mental and medical problems	
Condition	*Number of victims*
Dementia/memory loss	11
Mobility problems	10
Stroke	8
Heart problems	5
Incontinence	4
Speech problems	3
Mental health problems	2
Learning disability	2
Parkinson's disease	2
Sight problems	2
Alcohol problem	1
Amputee (leg)	1
Bowel problem	1
Chronic obstructive airways disease	1
Deafness	1
Diabetes	1
Liver disease	1
Multiple sclerosis	1
Osteoporosis	1

Note: It will be apparent that some men suffered multiple problems.

Other facts about male victims

Other important facts regarding male victims were:

- all 39 men were white

- 11 lived in residential care

- 8 lived alone

- 20 lived with the abuser.

The monitoring forms were designed so that social workers could give as much background information as possible about both the victim and the abuser. The amount of detail given by workers varied tremendously. Where information was scant, the researcher contacted the worker direct. It became clear that many workers had not obtained basic information, e.g. regarding age.

This lack of relevant recorded information may be regarded as symptomatic of the status of this work both administratively and professionally. There are few statutory duties in relation to these service-users; unlike the situations in Canada and the USA, few social services departments have designated sections for adult protection (in parallel with child protection). However, this is likely to change in the near future as the recommendations from *No Secrets: Guidance on Developing and Implementing Multi-agency Policies and Procedures to Protect Vulnerable Adults from Abuse* are implemented (Department of Health 2000a). Many social workers find work with older people distasteful and escape from doing it as much as they administratively can; training courses which in recent years have been strident in advocating anti-discriminatory practice do not extend the

moral value to considering the experiences of older people
and how to help them.

Abusers

In some cases information about the abuser was also
limited. This was because either the identity of the abuser
was unknown or the worker had failed to ask for details
about the abuser and had focused solely on the victim.

Gender

Here too we have to allow for the stereotype that most
abusers are men. Certainly previous research studies both
in regard to domestic violence and elder abuse support this.
In this project when considering the abusers of older
people in general, the majority of abusers were men (61 per
cent). However, in the cases where men were the victims of
abuse, there was a more equal divide. For this group there
were actually more female abusers (51 per cent): see Figure
2.6.

Figure 2.6 Gender of known abusers

Age

Figure 2.7 shows the ages of the known abusers. The youngest abuser was a male aged 22 years; the eldest abuser was a female aged 93 years.

Relationships

Again assumptions are often made that older people are mainly abused by a family member or someone who takes on the role of carer. Many definitions exclude abuse by strangers. Table 2.6 on the following page shows that the male victims were abused by a range of people and sometimes by more than one person: it will be noted that in 17 cases the abusers included people outside the family.

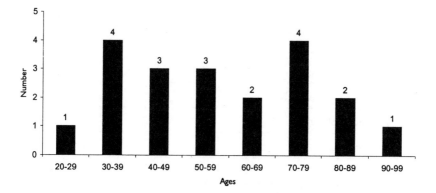

Figure 2.7 Ages of known abusers

Table 2.6 Relationship between male victims and abusers	
Abusers	*Number of cases*
Wife	8
Residential staff (group)	4
Son	4
Friend	3
Neighbour	3
Daughter	3
Residents	3
Member of staff in Home	2
Daughter-in-law	1
Granddaughter	1
Grandson	1
Other relative	1
Visitor	1
Niece and sister	1
Twin sons	1
Son and daughter-in-law	1
Son and nephew	1
Two strangers to the victim	1
NK	2

Types of elder abuse

As stated previously, workers were asked to complete monitoring forms using the definition of abuse as defined by the Social Services Inspectorate in 1993. They were asked to state which form of abuse had taken place:

- physical
- emotional
- financial
- neglect
- sexual.

Financial abuse was the most common form of abuse identified: 56 per cent of male victims had been financially abused and 46 per cent had been physically abused. Workers also identified that more than one-third of the men had been emotionally abused (see Table 2.7 and Figure 2.8).

Table 2.7 Types of abuse experienced	
Category of abuse	*Number of male victims*
Physical	18
Emotional	14
Financial	22
Neglect	7
Sexual	1

Twenty-three victims experienced only one type of abuse, eleven victims experienced two types of abuse, three victims experienced three types of abuse and two victims had experienced four types of abuse (see Table 2.8).

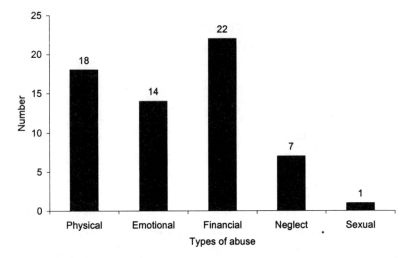

Figure 2.8 Elder abuse experienced by male victims

Table 2.8 Types and prevalence of abuse	
Category of abuse	*Number of victims*
Physical	8
Emotional	2
Financial	10
Neglect	3
Physical and emotional	4
Emotional and financial	4
Physical and financial	2
Financial and sexual	1
Physical, emotional and financial	1
Physical, financial and neglect	1
Emotional, financial and neglect	1
Physical, emotional, financial and neglect	2

The range and intensity of abuses suffered by male victims were similar to that suffered by women; the range of perpetrators was also similar. In other words, though fewer men proportionately are abused, those who are abused suffer in the same areas and to the same intensity as women.

CHAPTER 3

In-depth Interviews

Male interviewees

In-depth interviews were conducted with twelve male victims of elder abuse, aged between 60 and 80 years (see Tables 3.1 and 3.2) referred to the research project through day or resource centres. At the time of interview, three men were living in the community; the other nine had had emergency admissions into residential care because they had needed a place of safety.

The interviews lasted between 30 minutes and 2 hours; some men were interviewed on more than one occasion. This was because sometimes they became tired very easily (especially those who had been physically neglected and were very weak); others needed to keep talking about the abuse. The men were asked to talk about:

- their life
- abuse – their definition
- abuse they had experienced
- their needs
- the help and support received and its quality.

Their lives

When asked to talk about their lives, the men tended to focus on their early working life, the army and marriage. None of them spontaneously talked about their childhood, until prompted to do so.

Table 3.1 The interviewees				
Victim	*Age*	*Type of elder abuse*	*Abuser*	*Previous abuse*
Bert	68	FN	Son	
Colin	60	EF	Son	
David	70	F	Carers	CA
Fred	74	FN	Neighbours	
Gregory	79	FN	Carer	
Howard	79	PFN	Son	
Jim	76	PEFS	Wife	DV
Mac	76	PFN	Son and daughter	DV
Sam	62	PEFN	Wife and daughter	
Simon	68	PEFN	Twin sons	CA
Vernon	80	N	Wife	CA
William	79	PFNS	Friend	

Key to types of elder abuse

P =   physical
E =   emotional
F =   financial
N =   neglect
S =   sexual
CA =   child abuse
DV =   domestic violence

Table 3.2 Age of the men interviewed	
Age	*Number of men*
60–64	2
65–69	2
70–74	2
75–79	5
80–84	1

Earlier working life

With the exceptions of Fred and Jim, all the men still lived in the area where they had been born. Two had been professional men – David was a solicitor, Colin an accountant. William, Mac, Gregory and Vernon had worked in local industries – mining, steel, railway. Fred had been a rag-and-bone man. Jim said he had worked at so many jobs he became a 'real handy-man', employed by local firms. Simon had had a variety of jobs in order to support his children (e.g. taxi driver, publican) and had worked abroad as a draughtsman. Eleven of the men mentioned their army life at some point during interview. For Simon and Vernon going into the army was a way of 'escaping' from their families and unhappy childhoods. Jim had wanted to go into the navy, but had been refused on the grounds that he was partially deaf. He described himself as 'having always been a weakling'.

Hardship

None of the men interviewed had had an easy life; they all spoke of hardships they had experienced. Gregory had come to Britain as an immigrant and said he had 'a hard life'. He talked about the difficulties he had encountered in a country where the language and religion were different; he said people did not accept him. He still missed his family in Eastern Europe and had many unresolved issues.

Vernon talked about life after his mother had died when he was 11 years old. His father, whom he considered to be 'bad', brought in a housekeeper, but Vernon did not get on with her family. He was extremely unhappy and was glad to go into the army when he was 16 years old. He still feels resentment towards his father and cannot forgive him for his treatment. Vernon frequently talks in the survivors' group[1] about his father attending his wedding but walking out before the reception took place. He says he 'would never treat my own children like he has treated me'.

Marriage

Gregory was the only man not to have married; Fred and Howard had not married until they were in their thirties whereas the other men had married early in their adult lives. William, Simon, and Bert had been married twice. David, Bert and Simon had been divorced. At the time of interview Fred, William, Mac, Colin, Howard and Bert were widowed; Vernon and Sam were still married.

---

1   Two survivors' groups for older people have been set up as a result of the findings of the original research project. Four of the interviewed men have been involved in one of the groups – Bert, Jim, Vernon, William.

Losses

All the men had experienced some type of loss or bereavement during their lifetime and readily talked about this during interview. This will be discussed further when considering the men's needs: they clearly wanted or needed to speak of the losses and disappointments they had experienced earlier and later in their lives.

Types of elder abuse experienced

All twelve men had been victims of elder abuse and were able to talk about this quite openly. They were able to describe in detail exactly what had happened and how they felt about the abuse and the abuser. The most common form of abuse was financial, with neglect being almost as frequent (see Table 3.3).

Table 3.3 Types of abuse	
Category	*Number of victims*
Financial	11
Neglect	9
Physical	6
Emotional	4
Sexual	2

Eight men had been abused by family members; four men had been abused by people who were not related to them (see Table 3.4).

Table 3.4 Relationships between victims and abusers	
Abuser(s)	*Number of cases*
Son(s)	5
Daughter	2
Wife	3
Carer(s)	2
Friend	1
Neighbours	1

The descriptions used in Table 3.4 were the relationships as described by the victims themselves. Some men had been abused by more than one person. Mac had been abused by three different family members at different points in his life – wife, daughter and son. William was abused by a friend, whom he had known for many years and who became his wife's lover. Fred was taken advantage of by the next-door neighbours who said they would help him. David had gone to lodge with a young couple who acted as formal carers but then abused him. Like the women in the project, none of the victims was abused because their carer had become stressed. This supports the argument that elder abuse should not be seen only in terms of carer's stress; it is often a much more complex issue which needs to be investigated sensitively, as very often maintaining the relationship with the abuser is more important to the victim than stopping the abuse (Pritchard 2000).

Financial abuse

The most common type of abuse experienced by the men was financial, which supports the argument that abuse (both of men and of women) should be considered in a broad definition and context, not just in terms of physical and sexual violence. The men's vulnerability (which will be discussed below) made them an easy target for financial abuse. The majority had some form of illness (see Table 4.2 in next chapter) which made them dependent on others to collect pensions, to shop for them and to manage their finances generally.

William was registered as partially sighted and his wife, Ellen, was blind. Their friend Edmund obtained Ellen's signature on a number of documents which enabled him to draw money from her and William's accounts:

> You reckon it up…pension from the pit was turned over to him [Edmund]…she [Ellen] got £120 a week off me, that was cash in the purse and suddenly she had nothing left. So where has it gone?…I found out that he had bought these caravans and she had helped to pay for them and she'll not get a penny of that money now, as I have no witnesses. (William)

Colin had had a stroke and was housebound after he was discharged from hospital. His son insisted that Colin's money should be deposited in accounts in the bank where he worked. The son then controlled all transactions because he had access to the computer system and took possession of Colin's cashcard. His son also told everyone that his father was 'completely mad' having had the stroke and tried to obtain power of attorney through the Court of Protection.

Bert had cancer of the bowel and liver in the past and was terminally ill. When his wife died in 1999 he was persuaded to go to live with his son. Money started to 'disappear' from his bank account. His son had taken his cashcard and made withdrawals (totalling *c.* £3000) and he had also arranged for standing orders to be set up to pay rent for Bert's grandson (just under £1000 had been paid). Bert had no knowledge of this.

Gregory was housebound due to severe arthritis. A person he had known for years and who was also in her seventies travelled several miles every day 'to do for him'. She alleged that she cashed his pension, paid the bills and bought whatever he needed (food and clothes); she had complete control of his finances. It was clear on admission to care that she was not in fact buying things for him or paying the bills, because he had no clean clothes, and there was no water or electricity in the house. When staff asked her to buy some new slippers, she brought in old slippers which were dirty, stained and had holes in; staff threw them away.

Fred suffered with arthritis and had curvature of the spine. He was extremely lonely; his only company was his cat to whom he was devoted. The couple who lived next door to Fred took advantage of this situation. They offered to run errands for him, but in fact were taking money from him and stealing possessions from inside the house. The couple had also been drawing money out of his Post Office account. Fred was admitted to care just before Christmas when home care workers found that there was no food in the house and he had no money left.

Mac and Simon were financially abused because their abusers had addictions to drugs and needed to finance their habits. Mac was abused by his son, who was addicted to heroin and also had an alcohol problem. Similarly, Simon's twin sons drank heavily and used drugs:

> I think it's because they are on drugs…they like whisky, beer and strong lager…they get up in a morning drunk. (Simon)

They were also dealing in the local area. They brought friends and clients back to Simon's flat to use and sell drugs. All three abusers in these cases had criminal records for violent offences against other people in the community, not their own relatives.

Jim had always liked to buy his wife 'nice things' and continued to do so. Whenever he had been able to save any money, he had always spent it on buying his wife gifts. However, whatever he bought her it was 'never enough; she always wanted more'. He said in recent years 'money went to her head' when she started getting attendance allowance. After Jim left his wife the first time, he opened a separate bank account to protect his savings.

In all these cases, the abuse had been going on for a considerable length of time – from 6 months to 13 years; none of them was a one-off incident, so that considerable sums of money and possessions were stolen.

Neglect

When few policies existed on elder abuse, neglect tended to be put under the category of physical abuse, but it is now recognised that neglect can be physical or emotional. Recent guidance from the Department of Health defines neglect or acts of omission as:

> including ignoring medical or physical care needs, failure to provide access to appropriate health, social care or educational services, the withholding of the necessities of life, such as medication, adequate nutrition and heating. (Department of Health 2000a, p.9)

Workers often complain that it is difficult to identify neglect; but in the cases of the male victims identified, the neglect was very obvious. Yet it was only when it became extreme that some action was taken.

Physical neglect

What was astounding about the twelve men interviewed was that nine of them had been neglected; six were found to be in a gross state of neglect on admission to care. The men were extremely dirty and had obviously been wearing the same clothes for a very long time. Experienced care workers were 'shocked' at what they saw; some of their comments follow:

> William was said to 'look like a chimney sweep because the dirt is ingrained in his skin and his head is covered in blackheads'. When he was bathed, the water had to be changed several times because it kept turning black.

Gregory's 'skin was covered in green mould and his underpants were full of dried and fresh faeces. His genitals were red raw'. His hand was also swollen with an infection.

Howard 'looked like a hippy – his hair was really long and dirty'. He had fleas and lice.

Common features presented were:

- unwashed skin and/or ingrained dirt

- dirty, uncut finger and/or toe nails

- no teeth or badly fitting and/or stained dentures

- unwashed, uncombed hair

- dirty, torn clothes – no clean clothes available at home

- soiled underwear.

Some men were living in wholly unacceptable conditions. Bert had been forced to live in a room behind the garage where there were no cooking or washing facilities. He had special dietary requirements due to his ill-health. His son would send two meals a day out to him, but they were often not suitable. Bert said that he did not have all the equipment he required for his stoma care.

Both Gregory and Fred were said to be living in 'squalor' by their respective social workers who admitted them to care. A worrying fact about both of these cases was that home care services had been going into their homes for some time, but had not reported any concerns. On the day

Gregory came into care, it was found that there was no water supply (the toilet was completely overflowing), electricity or cooking facilities and that he had run out of coal for the fire. Fleas were found in the carpets and furniture; bedding was soiled and faeces were evident on the floor. Fred had been living in similar conditions. One accepts that standards differ between individuals, but it is incomprehensible how trained home care staff could have failed to report the conditions these men were living in. Maybe too often we hide behind the concepts of choice and self-determination. When these men were interviewed it was clear that they had not liked living in these conditions but had been unable to say this. Perhaps a fundamental form of abuse is that no one bothered to ask them how they felt and just assumed it was their choice to live this way. It is easy to stereotype men as not caring about how they live.

A commonality between these cases is that most of the victims were both financially abused and neglected at the same time. William and his wife, Ellen, had been 'cared for' by Edmund. Ellen had been having an affair with Edmund for many years; William had tolerated the situation for Ellen's sake, whom he loved dearly. As well as being financially abused, the couple also suffered gross neglect. William was admitted to a residential home for safety, while Ellen was admitted to hospital with pneumonia where she died. What upset William most was the fact that his wife had not been fed properly: 'He's done one meal a day for her and it's wrong'.

Another form of neglect includes 'ignoring medical or physical care needs, failure to provide access to appropriate health, social care or educational services' (Department of

Health 2000a, p.9). Howard suffered injuries after a house fire earlier in the year, but his son Neville refused to let his father have access to medical treatment. Prior to admission, Neville had also failed to allow his father to receive treatment to his injured arm, which was in fact broken.

Emotional neglect

Vernon was adamant that he was being neglected by his wife; day care staff said that he liked to be the centre of attention and felt that his wife was probably the victim rather than Vernon. Nevertheless, they took Vernon seriously because he truly believed that he was being abused. When interviewed, Vernon could explain why he felt that he was a victim. His wife goes out socially on a regular basis throughout the week. Vernon said he is often left alone for long periods of time and he does not like it. He believed that his wife should be there to keep him company. This is an interesting example regarding the problems of defining abuse. Social workers often identify abusive situations and feel frustrated when the victim sees this 'as normal'; whereas in the case of Vernon, workers did not see his situation as abusive, but he did.

Sam was emotionally neglected by both his wife and daughter. They insisted that he use only one room in the house; he was not allowed to watch television and they refused to talk to him. The only time he got any stimulation was when he attended the day centre once a week.

Below I shall discuss how many of the men were very isolated and consequently could be described as being emotionally neglected. The problem is – who has the responsibility for stimulating these men? No one legally.

Nevertheless, many of them had emotional needs that were neglected.

Physical abuse

Six men had been victims of physical abuse; most had been hit by the hands of their abusers rather than the use of implements:

> [they hit] with their hands. They think it's funny. (Simon)

> He hits me…with his hand and gives me a black eye too. (Howard)

> When you start talking to him he's as nice as pie and then he gets awkward…with his hands…knocked my bloody glasses off. (William)

Mac had been known previously to social services before a woman from the local area went in to see a duty social worker, on the day after an incident. The woman and her family had on the previous night seen Mac's son, Andrew, banging his father, who was in his wheelchair, into a wall and hitting him over the head.

Jim's wife regularly threatened to become physically violent and did so on occasions. Jim has a tracheotomy tube in his throat. His wife had gone to pull it out several times when she became angry; had she succeeded in doing this she could have killed Jim. When he left her on the second occasion, she became physically violent and had to be restrained by the police.

Emotional abuse

Four men said they had been the victims of emotional abuse. This was often in the form of name-calling or ridiculing the victim's condition. Colin, who had had a stroke, constantly talked about the names which his son had repeatedly called him. After the stroke, his son said he was 'brain-dead', 'mad', 'incapable' and 'fit for nothing'. He tried to convince both Colin and the professionals working with him that he was mentally ill as a result of the stroke. He also denied him access to his grandson, who was not allowed to visit his grandfather any more.

Simon, who had had a heart attack and suffered with Parkinson's Disease, was also a victim of ridicule. His twin sons used to laugh at him as they were hitting him: 'they think it's funny'.

Jim's wife was a very argumentative person, who constantly shouted and screamed at him. When he was admitted to a place of safety for the second time, staff themselves became victims to her abusive behaviour. She was verbally abusive on the telephone when she was told Jim did not want to speak to her and she presented as being very aggressive when she arrived at the door of the resource centre and was denied access to her husband. Other professionals had witnessed her emotionally abusing Jim when they were living together. She had also threatened to attack the social worker physically after she removed Jim to a place of safety the first time.

While talking about the emotional abuse, some victims also talked about the control their abuser exercised over them. William talked about how Edmund tried to control his life by telling him what he could and could not do:

He says 'You mustn't go away from this house'. So I said 'I can go where I want, I don't have to ask you where I want to go', so I took my hook. (William)

When William did leave the house, Edmund called the police to report him missing and he was brought back.

Colin felt that his son had completely taken over his life and that he had no control at all; he felt completely powerless. This was very hard for Colin, who had been an accountant until very recently. He felt he had lost everything.

Sexual

Only since the mid-1990s has any significant attention been given to adult men as victims of sexual abuse. For example, literature exists regarding violence and abuse within gay relationships (Appleby and Anastas 1998; Farley 1992; Island and Letellier 1991; Landholt and Dutton 1997). However, the sexual abuse of adult men, whether by male or female perpetrators, still remains very much a taboo subject. Both Jim and William disclosed that they had been sexually abused.

Jim was sexually abused by his wife, who told him that he was 'useless in bed' and told their GP that Jim 'did not do his duty enough'. She forced him into sexual activity after he chose to move into a single bed. He had said to her he did not want sex after he had cancer and his pelvis was painful.

William disclosed he had been sexually abused by Edmund, who was a known Schedule 1 offender.[2] He had

2   Someone who has been sentenced for committing a crime against a child (from Children and Young Persons Act 1933).

physically abused William and forced him into sexual activities with himself and prostitutes.

Previous abuse

During the in-depth interviews, the men were invited to talk about their earlier life experiences. Five men disclosed that they had been abused in earlier life. Simon had been physically abused by his father from an early age; his father had also abused his mother:

> He was vicious…my mum used to say 'Oh you're not going to hit him again'. He never said he was sorry. (Simon)

Despite this, when Simon divorced his first wife, he entrusted his parents with the care of his five children when he went out to work:

> I divorced their mother in 1962, when they [the twins who abused him] were 3 months old. My mother brought them up…I had three jobs. I just worked all the time. (Simon)

David had been physically and emotionally abused by his father, who was a strong disciplinarian and favoured his two daughters. Vernon had been emotionally abused and neglected by his father and housekeeper after his mother died.

Both Jim and Mac fitted into the category of 'battered husband syndrome' (Steinmetz 1978). They had previously been abused physically by their wives, but both of them maintained that they had had happy marriages. Mac saw having arguments as 'just normal'. It was also known that he and his wife had previously been cared for by his daughter, who had physically and financially abused both her parents as well as neglecting them.

All the men interviewed had a sense of resignation about what had happened to them, whether the abuse had been experienced in the past or very recently. None of them presented as embittered but rather with a sense of sadness.

I have no complaints. (Howard)

CHAPTER 4

Needs of Male Victims

One of the main aims of the in-depth interviews was to ascertain the scope of the needs of male victims of elder abuse. The men were asked to talk about their past and current needs; most of them tended to focus on the present as 'nothing can be done about the past'. Yet for some of them there were many unresolved issues. The findings indicate that male victims had similar needs to female victims (Pritchard 2000), but the men gave more importance to certain particular needs, and this will be discussed in this chapter. Table 4.1 summarises the key needs which were identified by the men themselves.

Vulnerability

Before discussing the needs as identified by the men themselves, some attention must be paid to their vulnerability. A key issue (as mentioned previously) was the fact that all the men were easy targets for abusers. In the guidance *No Secrets* produced by the Department of Health (2000a) the definition of vulnerable adult is taken from the consultation paper *Who Decides?* issued by the Lord Chancellor's Department (1997):

...may be in need of community care services by reason of mental or other disability, age or illness; and who is or may be unable to take care of him or herself, or unable to protect him or herself against significant harm or exploitation. (Department of Health 2000a, p.9)

Table 4.1 Summary of needs as described by the victims
• advice
• assessment of medical problems
• assessment of mental capacity
• company
• maintaining contact with social worker
• management of finances
• permission to talk
• personal safety
• physical/basic care
• place of safety
• police involvement
• practical help
• protection of the abuser
• reconciliation with family
• rehousing or permanent accommodation
• remain loyal and do one's duty
• talk about abuse
• talk about/deal with losses

All the men interviewed fitted this definition of being vulnerable. The majority had poor physical health and/or needed help with basic care. Table 4.2 lists the key medical and physical problems of each victim.

Table 4.2 Physical and medical problems	
Bert:	ileostomy; metastatic bowel and liver malignancy; ascites
Colin:	stroke; short-term memory loss; depression
David:	alcohol misuse; slight confusion
Fred:	arthritis; curvature of the spine; slight confusion
Gregory:	arthritis; doubly incontinent
Howard:	Parkinson's disease
Jim:	tracheotomy; partially deaf; cancer
Mac:	emphysema; breathing problems; slight confusion
Sam:	stroke; poor mobility; slight confusion
Simon:	previous heart attack; Parkinson's Disease
Vernon:	stroke; mobility affected
William:	frail; partially sighted

Another causal factor of abuse was the fact that most of the men were extremely lonely, so welcomed company or help from people outside. Subsequently, carers were able to take advantage of the situation. David, who had never lived alone during his lifetime, lodged with a young couple who provided a room and meals for him. David's son refused to have anything to do with his father, because of a previous alcohol problem. Fred welcomed the company of the young couple who lived next door and offered to run errands for him. They and home care staff were the only contacts he had with the outside world.

Three other men were abused by family members, who were considered to be the main carers. Mac was abused by his son, who had an alcohol problem and an addiction to heroin; he came to live with his father after his mother died. Sam had a stroke which left him weak physically; he was completely controlled by his wife and daughter. Similarly, Colin, after his stroke, was 'managed' by his son, who took control of every aspect of Colin's life.

Jim's view of himself made him vulnerable. His self-esteem is extremely low and he constantly says of himself 'I've always been a weakling'; this stems from having been ill during childhood and having to attend an 'open school' and also being rejected by the navy on health grounds. He presents as a very passive and kind man, who would not fight back. Consequently, it was probably very easy for his wife to take control and exert her power over him.

Place of safety

Nine men had been admitted to emergency placements, either to hospital in the first instance (Mac and Howard) or to a resource centre. Howard was probably the only victim who did not see the need or want to leave home. This will be discussed further below when considering the principles of self-determination and choice. Each man had come into care via a different route, though all the initial referrals had come to social services departments:

- **Bert** was helped by his sister; they went to see a duty social worker together. Bert said he wanted to get out of his son's home.

- **David**, who had been a solicitor, referred himself: 'Because I knew the system, I rang social services to get me out'

- **Fred** was admitted as an emergency before Christmas when home care staff found there was no food or money in the house.

- **Gregory** was admitted to care on the first day he came for day care as the staff at the centre were horrified at his state of neglect.

- Neighbours contacted the police (who contacted social services) when they knew that **Howard** had hurt his arm and suggested he had been hit by his son; they were also concerned about Howard's state of neglect and general mistreatment by his son.

- **Jim** told the district nurse, who visited every day, that he wanted to leave. She contacted social services and he was admitted to a place of safety. This happened on two occasions.

- **Mac** was admitted to hospital after the couple who had witnessed him being physically abused in the street went to see a duty social worker.

- **Simon** had initially sought help from his daughter and sister, who lived in other cities; they contacted social services.

- **William** came into care when his wife was admitted to hospital and it was thought he could not cope on his own; Edmund, the friend and carer, did not live with the couple.

Only four men had made the conscious decision to leave (Bert, David, Jim and Simon). The others had come in as emergencies because relatives, neighbours or workers had concerns for their well-being and safety. All of them came in willingly, although in Howard's case he did not really understand what was happening to him. His account of what happened to him is quite frightening; he was picked up off the street by the police who had been contacted by the neighbours:

> I was going shopping. I was going across the crossing and what stopped first was a police car and they said they would ring for the social worker....I was sat down [in a shop] and waited until they came and I got off the chair and went with them [social workers]... they took me to the hospital and did an X-ray and when it came out it was broke...[after an operation] then the nurse got me clothes and they didn't say where I was going and I was in the ambulance and then it turned up here [resource centre]....I thought what is this place and when I sat down I found out what it was. (Howard)

The social workers who were involved genuinely believe that they had explained everything to Howard and I am sure that they did. But the point is whether enough 'checking out' was done with him to ascertain whether he really did understand what was happening to him. From what he said in the research interview, it was clear he had not understood at the time. It is important that victims are not rushed to make decisions or to fit in with the worker's busy schedule. Time must be taken to explain what is going to happen; otherwise the process which should be helpful actually becomes abusive.

All the placements had been arranged very quickly; there were no delays and the men (with the exception of Howard) felt that speed had been helpful. Jim's second escape had to be well planned. As on the first occasion Jim had told the district nurse that he wanted to leave; she in turn had contacted the social worker. Jim's wife had threatened to kill the social worker if she ever came near her again, because she had been the one who had admitted Jim to a place of safety on the first occasion. It was arranged that several people would go to get Jim out – the police, the social worker and her manager, a worker from the resource centre. Jim's wife refused to let them in at first, but the police officer said he had the right of entry. Jim and his wife talked with the others present, but then she became aggressive, tried to attack Jim and had to be physically restrained.

The majority of the men were happy with their emergency accommodation apart from Mac and William, who said they did not like being 'with strangers'. This is an important point for assessment; not every individual likes to be placed in a group setting. In some circumstances it is unavoidable, but steps should be taken to find out whether there are other alternatives, for example, temporary accommodation with friends or relatives.

Continued or regular contact

There was evidence in some cases of men being 'dumped' in a place of safety and then having little contact with the worker who had placed them. It is usually expected that a review meeting or case conference will take place soon after admission. Generally, the men's experience was that they did not know what was going to happen or there were long time gaps. Howard talked about his case conference experience:

> Well they had a meeting, the housing, the police. I had the third degree and someone was taking down notes and I told them then 'I want to go straight home', so they are going to have another meeting [three months after admission]. (Howard)

Communication was often bad between the fieldworker and care staff. Care staff felt frustrated with many social workers because of the lack of information about the victim given at the time of placement and/or after admission, and because of lack of information and updates about the abuse investigation.

There were some examples of where the social worker did not follow up on problems which needed to be sorted out quickly. In William's case, the pension and bank books remained in the house to which the abuser had a key. William became very agitated about getting these books from the house:

She [social worker] hasn't told me nothing. That's why I want to know. I have two weeks to come [pension]. Will I get it? (William)

The social worker did not visit William for days after admission and told care staff she expected them to make contact with the bank and solicitor 'to sort things out'. The staff did not see this as their responsibility. The books remained in William's house for weeks. This did not help William's agitation. It is crucial that problems which are important to the victim are given some priority; situations should not be allowed to drift. There also needs to be some clarity about roles and responsibilities; this should be done through the case conference process. Another problem is that workers do not always follow procedure; that is to say, case conferences are not always convened within the time limit stated within the policy and procedural documents.

Bert was also a victim of poor practice and bad communication. He was initially placed in one resource centre but had two subsequent moves which were experienced as very disruptive to him. When he moved between resource centres and hospital there was a total lack of communication and sharing of information. The social worker should be at the pivotal point of planning and information, but this certainly was not the case for Bert.

One of the aims of resource centres is to provide emergency accommodation which should be a short-term measure. Because some of the social workers let things drift, these were in fact long placements for some of the men, in particular David and Howard. Most men really enjoyed staying in the resource centres, which are very different from a residential home. A worry is that some of the men made decisions about going into care permanently based on their experience of the resource centre. Good practice would say that they should visit their new home before admission, but some of them were not given this opportunity. Some had become very settled at the resource centre and it was disorientating for them when they moved. David's mental state deteriorated rapidly when he was first placed permanently in a home. Over time, it improved again.

Rehousing and permanent accommodation

With the exception of Howard, none of the men who had been admitted into a place of safety wanted to return to the abusive situation; hence there was a need for new accommodation. With the exceptions of Bert, Jim and Simon, who were given flats, and Howard, who is still in his emergency placement at the time of writing (eleven months after admission), the majority were placed permanently in a residential or nursing home. However, this presented problems for some of the men.

William definitely did not want to go into permanent care; he wanted to live in a place of his own:

> Well I would like a little bungalow on my own. I know where I am then....All I want is a house on my own and I shall be satisfied. (William)

Staff in the resource centre believed that William would be able to live in the community with home care support. The social worker, who had had little contact with William, strongly disagreed. Care staff argued that they had been able to assess William correctly because they were working very closely with him. At the case review the chair of the meeting (who was the social worker's line manager) agreed that William should be placed in residential care. This went against his wishes:

I won't go. I have my own mind. I won't go. (William)

William was placed in a nursing home. The care staff felt that their assessment of William had been totally ignored by both the social worker and line manager. It also caused a great deal of discussion in the resource centre about how care staff are undervalued and not taken seriously when presenting their assessments.

Alternative accommodation is an ongoing issue for Vernon, who continues to live with his wife. For a long time he has thought about going into residential care, but feels this would be a huge step. He talks about this a great deal in the survivors' group and the general consensus of group members is that residential care would not be appropriate for Vernon. He would be suited to sheltered accommodation and is currently thinking about this. The survivors' group provides a forum for Vernon where he can verbalise his thoughts and he is not being forced to make a quick decision.

Personal safety

Once a victim is in a place of safety it is necessary to ensure that steps are taken to offset the risk of future harm. The victim (and care staff) may be fearful of the abuser trying to gain access. There can be fears that the abuser may be physically violent if he or she visits the unit (which can be frightening for the victim, other service users, and staff) or that the abuser may try to intimidate the victim – maybe trying to persuade him to return home, withdraw allegations and so on.

Mac's son, who was known to have a criminal record for violent offences, regularly rang the resource centre and was verbally abusive to staff, accusing them of neglecting his father and being 'a centre for euthanasia'.

When Jim left his wife on the first occasion, she started visiting him and putting pressure on him to return home. Eventually he relented and went home for Christmas because 'she promised she'd change'. A month later he left again and went to another place of safety, where she was verbally abusive to the staff.

Another important issue regarding the safety of service users came up just before Simon was admitted as an emergency. There had been staffing problems in the kitchen of the resource centre and a chef had to be brought in from a local employment agency. Many things started to go missing from the kitchen and from the resource centre. It came to light that it was the temporary chef who was stealing and he left. The chef had a very unusual surname. Within days Simon was admitted as an emergency placement. Staff could not believe that he also had the same strange surname as the chef who had left. It turned out the chef was one of Simon's twin sons. This raises the issue about undertaking police checks for people who are going to work with vulnerable adults. In the UK this is not ordinarily done. Simon's twin sons had criminal records for violent offences. If police checks had been undertaken as a matter of routine, the chef probably would not have been employed. It is frightening to think what may have happened if Simon had been placed in a so-called safe place and then come face to face with one of his abusers. Simon was very clear about how he felt about his sons and what he wanted to happen:

> Very annoyed... I just want to keep them away. (Simon)

Simon's personal safety was an ongoing issue. He did not want his sons to know where he was going to live, so it was important that everyone involved was aware of this and kept his address confidential.

Permission to talk

It is generally thought that men find it difficult to admit that they have been abused. I was particularly struck by the way in which all the men talked openly about their lives and the abuse they had experienced. They seemed very much at ease with me when disclosing what had happened to them. Their willingness to talk may have been due to the fact that they were aware of my role; that is, they knew that I was running focus groups and that I work with victims of abuse. Like the female victims, it was important for them to know that they had permission to speak and were going to be believed, not ridiculed (Pritchard 2000). This was probably even more important to the men for whom it must be hard to admit that they have been abused, when society normally sees men less in the role of victim than as perpetrator.

In talking about abusive experiences, I asked the men if it made a difference or problem for them in my being female and whether they would prefer to talk to a man. All said it did not make any difference; what was important to them was that 'someone is willing to listen'. The majority of them had female social workers and none of them objected or had any complaints about this.

Nevertheless, in normal social situations most of the men did enjoy the company of other male residents to talk about 'man things'. This was a specialised need. They had a lot in common, having lived and worked in the same area. Often there is a predominance of females in residential settings. On occasions when there were quite a few men in residence, they tended to congregate together in one area (not designated for this purpose). David spent most of his time in a small television/smoking room and particularly enjoyed the company of the other men, who tended to meet up in this room. When he was placed permanently in a nursing home, he continued the same pattern and made a close male friend with whom he spent a great deal of time. Bert was admitted during the summer months and spent most of the day with other men sitting outside the resource centre under a parasol. Howard always sat with a group of men in a certain part of the resource centre; he rarely engaged with the females.

Two men, Colin and Vernon, needed to continue to talk about what was happening to them, because they both remained in their abusive situations. Colin refused help from professionals, who he felt were 'taking sides' with his son. Also because he had always been in control of his life and had had a 'responsible' job he wanted to sort things out for himself. His need was to be able to talk; he did not want anyone else to take action. He spent hours on the telephone talking to a few select friends whom he felt he could trust. These friends became very frustrated as the number of phone calls increased, because Colin just wanted to talk and would not accept advice or practical help.

Vernon talked openly about his situation when he attended the day centre twice a week, but he also attended the survivors' group which he found 'good' because 'I can talk to you and you listen'. Day care staff thought that Vernon was attention seeking and liked to be the centre of interest, but in the survivors' group he took an active role in trying to encourage a female survivor to talk about her experiences; this woman was reluctant to engage in discussion but wanted to attend the group just to listen. Vernon was very supportive towards her:

What's going on in your head? It helps to talk. (Vernon)

What was also often evident during interviews was that there was no bitterness about what had happened, but rather a sense of resignation. None of the men apportioned blame to others.

I only have myself to blame. (David)

And when asked if it helped to talk about what had happened David acknowledged that the resource centre was 'a godsend'; he believed that no one could help him and followed the philosophy:

Physician – heal thyself. (David)

In some cases, the victim presented as emotionally flat; this was particularly so in the case of William, who did not show any emotion about the fact that his wife had been having an affair with his friend. The only thing he felt strongly about was the fact that his wife had been neglected; he was not angry about his own abuse:

> I couldn't do a thing about me. I told her about him but she didn't take any notice. (William)

Assessment

All the men who were admitted to a place of safety needed to be fully assessed. In theory this should have been part of the adult abuse investigation.

Medical

The majority of male victims needed some type of medical assessment. All had had health problems in the past and some had ongoing conditions which needed attention (see Table 4.2). Those who had been physically neglected should have had thorough medical checks, but this was not done routinely. GPs were contacted to deal with specific problems (for example Gregory's green mould on his skin and swollen hand), rather than for a general check on the long-term effects of neglect. Care staff drew up care plans in order to 'build up' or 'fatten up' the victims.

Mental

Prior to interview there were concerns about the mental capacity of five of the men: staff had questioned whether some of them were confused or suffering with dementia. It is a matter for concern that jargon terms regarding a person's mental state are often bandied about. On case files

I read statements about 'dementia' or 'Alzheimer's Disease', when in fact no real assessment of capacity had been undertaken. It is dangerous practice to make assumptions about a person's mental state. Some of the men interviewed were slightly confused, but with the use of skilled interviewing and communication techniques they were able to tell their stories very clearly. The slight confusion could have been a result of the abuse or of the move to an unfamiliar place. In two cases (Mac and William) where the men were very slightly confused, entries had been made on their files that they were suffering with 'severe dementia', which was definitely not true in either case. (Mac at the time of admission was suffering with a chest infection.) On admission it was questioned whether David was 'suffering with Alzheimer's', but when a full assessment had been undertaken it was concluded that his alcohol abuse was causing his slight confusion, not Alzheimer's Disease. This highlights the need for proper assessment of mental capacity and it should be remembered that an indicator of abuse can be temporary confusion. Even the men who were slightly confused were able to tell their stories to me and because I saw most of them on a regular basis, I knew that they were consistently giving me the same information and detail.

In contrast, staff had not detected that Bert's mental state was not as it should be. He could understand and respond to questions, but what became very evident in interview was that he was presenting some signs typical of a dementia. He was repetitive and obsessional about numbers; he constantly repeated his army and bus conductor's numbers and seemed to enjoy talking about the killings he had done while in the army. My first thought was that the problems with memory could be a result of the cancer spreading to the brain. When checking his file, a report was found which had been prepared at an earlier time by a community psychiatric nurse, who had noted the same patterns, but this had not been followed up. Another concern was that workers in the resource centres where he had been placed, together with the social worker, were speculating about his life expectancy. I was initially told that 'someone said he has three months to live'. Information was being bandied about without a definite prognosis from his consultants. Again there was a lack of co-ordination and communication between the people involved. When I asked Bert about his health he told me that he was fine and the cancer had been dealt with. In the following week after interview, the palliative care team were contacted and started to work with Bert. He then started to attend the survivors' group and we were able to talk openly about his impending death.

Other assessment issues

In some cases assessments need to be undertaken in relation to the abuser, as part of the risk assessment on behalf of the victim. A basic question should be: 'Is the victim at risk of harm if he returns home?' In Howard's case everyone was worried about his son, Neville, who had been known previously to mental health services. There had been concerns about Neville since he was a child; he was thought to be 'educationally subnormal' and had attended a special school. In his teenage years he was excluded from school after mutilating pet rabbits and incidents of bullying. There were also concerns in adulthood. Neville made inappropriate sexual suggestions to women in the local area (the community were aware that he had stalked several women and had previously served time in a remand centre) and Howard in interview referred to more recent incidents:

> But the other year he started taking photographs of women ... then he stopped taking them and he was going to start again and somebody put the spoke in about it. (Howard)

When Howard was admitted to a place of safety, the social worker tried to involve the community mental health team involved but they refused. In effect, Howard became a victim of the system. His social worker felt that it was too dangerous for him to go home without Neville being supported by someone from the mental health team. As well as risks of physical harm, there were also concerns about the squalid conditions within the home. Neville himself had not washed for eleven years, since the day his mother died. The situation continues to drag on at the time of writing. Howard is a very passive man and will agree to what is put to him. He is not able to assert himself. This case is a prime example of where workers have 'rescued' the victim and the fears of the workers are overriding the wishes of the victim to return home.

Loyalty and duty

For some men it was important 'to remain loyal and to abide by your duty'. Howard had a high sense of duty towards his son, Neville:

I'm his father. I have to help him. (Howard)

He felt it was his duty to provide a home, do the shopping, pay the bills and so on; he did not think there was anything wrong with the fact that Neville contributed nothing towards running the household.

William was similarly loyal and dutiful to his wife. Even though she had been having an affair with Edmund for many years, he felt that he had to protect her. It was known that Edmund was a Schedule 1 offender but William did not think his wife should be informed and needed to be protected from this knowledge:

> He got sent to jail for messing about with kids....We didn't think we could tell her...well her nerves were bad at the time. (William)

Protecting the abuser(s)

In a few cases the victims wanted the police to be involved and this will be discussed below. However, it was very important to most of the men to act in ways which protected the abuser. As noted above, none of the men showed malice towards the abuser and did not want to take legal action, even when they were not related. David, who was abused by his carers, said:

> I didn't ring the police because they have a 5-year-old boy and I didn't want anything to happen to them. (David)

Fred, who lost hundreds of pounds, possessions and food to his neighbours, was living in squalor, was malnourished and had few possessions left. However, he insisted that the couple had been good to him:

She was a right nice woman. (Fred)

Other men felt loyalty towards family members. William, who was totally accepting of the fact that his wife had been having an affair for years, presented as being emotionally flat and depressed:

You are better off dead when you are like me. (William)

What angered him was that his wife had not been fed properly and he could not get access to his pension book or bank account:

He's done one meal a day for her and it's wrong...I played hell with him for only giving her one meal a day. It needs sorting out...I want the money; I worked in the pit all them years for nothing. (William)

Loyalty and duty were important and this affected decisions about action against the abuser. Howard's son, Neville, had always lived at home and had never worked; he was aged 46 at the time of the interview. He had started to hit his father when there were problems about his benefit claim. Neville did not pay rent to his father or make any contribution towards the bills:

Well he pays his bills what he owes...he has Sky [cable television] to pay and clothes for himself he pays that monthly. He got a credit card, well he got two – one for Barclays Bank and one for the Scottish. So he packed the Scottish up and kept Barclays. He has been told he can't have any more. He has to pay so much a month and he pays the club so much. (Howard)

Sorting out practical matters

The men come from a generation where males and females were seen to have specific roles: the man was seen as the 'breadwinner', 'head of the household'. Stemming from this attitude, it was important to the male victims of elder abuse to take back control from the abuser and to sort out very practical matters for themselves. The practical problems needed sorting quickly, because otherwise delay generated more anxiety for the victim. Very often possessions needed to be collected from the household.

Bert needed his stoma care equipment from his room and he also wanted his possessions. The social worker made an appointment to pick up these things but when she got there, all she could collect was the stoma equipment and one pair of glasses because the son had thrown everything else away. From that point on, Bert always walked around holding the things which he had left and were important to him – for example cigarettes and bus pass.

William was very frustrated that his pension book remained at home, where the abuser could have access to it. The social worker did nothing to obtain the book during a three-week period and expected the residential staff to make contact with the bank and solicitor on behalf of William. It is important to victims that things are sorted out quickly and not left to drag on. Assumptions should not be made that there is no urgency simply because the victim is in a place of safety.

In contrast, Fred's social worker responded quickly to his concerns about his cat, who was probably the most important thing to him in the world. Placement of a cat may not seem like a matter of urgency, but to Fred it was. The cat needed feeding when he was admitted to care, but then an alternative home needed to be found when Fred went permanently into a residential care, because the home would not accept the cat.

These two cases show how workers' practices vary and affect the service which victims receive. As an exemplar of genuine care, Fred's social worker visited him very regularly – on a daily basis when he was first admitted – and communicated by telephone regularly with care staff. In some other cases, it is a concern that victims of abuse do not receive a consistent provision of service. Too much is left to the luck of an individual worker's attitudes and practices. Some workers look only at short-term remedies like finding a place of safety, and provide no ongoing support or planning for the longer term.

Advice

Most of the men were clear about what they wanted to happen in the future and how they wanted to lead their lives. However, most had certain problems which required them to seek advice from professionals. These needs were mainly in relation to:

- housing

- finances

- legal matters.

Table 4.3 shows the specific subject areas about which advice required as stated by the men and the sources of help.

Table 4.3 Advice	
Specific advice needed on	*Source of help*
alternative accommodation	social worker, housing officer
gaining access to pension book,cashcard, bank accounts, insurance policies	bank or building society manager, solicitor
future management of finances	bank or building society manager, solicitor
obtaining a divorce	solicitor

It was important to take control again and manage their own affairs:

> I would like a little bungalow on my own. I know where I am then. I am on my own now. If they leave me alone I will make it. (William)

Normal practice was for the social worker to liaise with the housing department to provide alternative accommodation. This was done very carefully in the cases of Simon, who needed to be rehoused away from his twin sons, and for Jim, who needed to be distanced from his wife.

The men who had been financially abused had little knowledge what steps needed to be taken to safeguard their assets. There was little knowledge about freezing accounts or changing joint accounts. Information from managers in banks or building society was crucial. Where possible, it was important to maintain the man's independence in handling such matters. If he could travel to meet with a manager this was preferable to the social worker 'taking over and doing it all'. It was important to Bert while he was staying in the resource centres to be able to have an appointment with the bank manager, and also for someone to escort him to cash his pension and buy his cigarettes for himself once a week. It was important to empower the men so that they could take control of their lives again. If the victim cannot go out for whatever reason, arrangements should ideally be made for the professional to visit the victim.

Solicitors became involved with some of the men, who wanted to sort things out 'in a legal way'. When the police failed to intervene in Bert's situation where money had been taken and standing orders set up fraudulently, Bert and his social worker went to see a solicitor, who agreed to act on his behalf. Sam went on his own to see a solicitor about getting a divorce from his wife and finding a place to live. William had been to a solicitor before being admitted to care and wanted to go again, but the social worker failed to arrange this.

Company

All the men were isolated either physically or emotionally. As already mentioned, some were living in situations where they had little contact with the outside world apart from their abusers. The exceptions were Vernon and Mac. Vernon was taken to the local working men's club by his daughter and attended day centre twice a week. Nevertheless, he still saw himself as 'lonely' when his wife left him alone in the house during the day. Mac also left the house when his son took him out for a drink. Sam, who was kept in one room by his wife and daughter, was 'let out' only when he came to day centre; he did 'sneak out' once to seek advice from a solicitor about obtaining a divorce. The others remained 'housebound' in the sense that they had no social contacts.

Once admitted to a place of safety, David, Fred and Sam welcomed contact with other people and the chance to talk. As already noted, David spent most of his time in the television/smoking room with other men. Fred particularly liked to talk to staff rather than the other residents and he also became very dependent on his social worker, who visited him very regularly; care staff felt he was almost 'obsessional' about her, but Fred saw her as the person who had helped him. Sam attended day care once a week and told everyone about how his wife and daughter made him live in one room and would not let him watch television.

William and Mac did not like being in their temporary placements 'with strangers'. Mac was placed in a unit where he had attended for day care, but he still did not like it. They both wanted to be in their own homes. Colin was living at home and was lonely, but refused outside help from anyone.

Losses and bereavement

All the men had experienced loss or bereavement during their lifetimes (see Table 4.4 on the next page) and some of them had a continuing need to talk about this. Jim had thirteen siblings, all of whom are now dead. He remembers particularly his older brother, who was killed in the Second World War. Between the ages of 10 and 13 Jim had attended an 'open school' because of ill-health. The day he returned to 'normal school' he heard his brother had 'been blown to bits'.

Table 4.4 Types of loss
• death of siblings, parents, wives, close friends
• loss of contact with particular family members e.g. children
• loss of money or savings
• loss of personal control over one's life
• loss of abilities e.g. mobility, speech, memory

Few of the men had ever been given the opportunity to vent their feelings, perhaps because it is not seen as a macho thing to do. A common need for all the men was to maintain contact with particular family members.

Even though the men had spent most of their lives in the same local area, many had lost contact with friends and family. Because of their isolation, some were not informed when a relative had died and were upset when they eventually heard of the death:

One sister she died in July. I didn't know nothing about it. Nobody told me anything about it. They cremated her. I don't even know today what she died with. (William)

Six of the men were widowed and welcomed the opportunity to talk about their wives. Fred, Bert and Howard still missed their wives greatly and wanted to talk about their deaths. Bert's second wife had died of cancer; it was important for him to talk about the details of this, especially as his own death became imminent. Bert also needed to talk about the loss of contact with his six children; he said his wife had 'poisoned' them against him when they divorced. He had had no contact with them until recently when he found them again. He was angry because he felt that the children were not looked after properly when they were younger:

> She and her mother earnt money in the back of the car then spent it on holidays to Gran Canaria rather than the children who went without. (Bert)

Colin was both upset and angry that his son would not allow his grandson to visit after he had his stroke.

When David was admitted to care, his son would not visit him but his daughter-in -law did. She informed staff that her husband was very angry with his father because he had had a drink problem and been violent towards him in the past. When this was discussed in interview, David talked about his life and why he had turned to drink. He felt that his father had always favoured his two sisters, who were 'given everything'. David had wanted to train as a barrister, but his father said it would cost too much, so David went into his father's firm of solicitors. Their partner then stole money from the firm, which went bankrupt, and David was forced to go to work as a prosecutor for the Crown; he felt he had been capable of 'better things'. On top of that his marriage failed and he returned to live with his father, whom he hated.

Gregory had left all his family in Eastern Europe. He talked about not knowing whether his family were really blood relatives or whether he had been adopted. It was something that was continuing to bother him but could not be resolved as he had no idea where his family lived and he did not want to make any contact with other people from his country who lived locally.

Cultural needs

Gregory was the only interviewee who had been born outside the UK. He came from an Eastern European country and it was clear that certain of his cultural needs had not been identified or met. His country had been invaded by Russia when he was 20 years old. It was at this time Gregory came to live in England. He had led a very solitary life and had no family in England. He had always worked but has no friends now.

Gregory understands what is said to him, but still finds it difficult to talk in English. When the social worker came to discuss his future care, she brought with her a Russian interpreter because it was 'the nearest to his country'. This was probably one of the worst things she could have done as Gregory had come to England to escape from the Russians. Sadly she had done nothing to find out about his level of communication or understanding of English or about the history relating to his background and country. All she wished to ascertain was whether he wanted to go into residential care on a permanent basis. This social worker, like many others, was 'under pressure to get things sorted'. Practical matters seemed to take precedence, but surely emotional needs should be equally important. If the social worker had taken time to get some background information, she could have found an appropriate interpreter from a city nine miles away.

The social worker claimed she was 'too busy' to ring round to get any information. It was only through the care staff taking the initiative and asking how to get this information from other sources that any headway was made. They did this without the help of the social worker:

- information about the country, its history, customs and religion was found on the Internet

- one enquiry to another social services department located an association which could help people from Gregory's country.

Gregory did agree to go into residential care but was then left to wait. The care staff became very frustrated because they felt that 'nothing was happening' as the weeks drifted by. There was no contact between the social worker and Gregory while he waited to find out what was going to happen to him. When he was finally placed, it happened with a day's notice over a weekend. Many care staff were upset because they had not had the chance to say 'goodbye' to Gregory.

By spending time with Gregory it was possible to find out what was important to him. He appeared to be a very lonely man who missed his family. He had unresolved issues regarding whether he was 'adopted'. Religion was very important to him. All of these needs could be identified and support provided in coping with them in the long term. But sadly there were no plans to do so.

Police involvement

Workers often assume that victims do not want to involve the police in taking proceedings because of the wish to protect the abuser. As a result social workers sometimes do not ask the direct question whether the victim does or does not want to involve the police:

> I have not directly asked him whether he wants to pursue the allegation. (Social worker)

Some of the men definitely did want the police involved but the response from the police was sometimes poor.

Bert was angry that his money had been stolen. A police officer from the Domestic Violence Unit had been invited to attend the case conference, but sent her apologies. There was a recommendation that the police should be contacted again. A police constable from the local police station came to see the social worker in the first instance:

> He took details of Bert's situation and recommended Bert seeks a solicitor's advice as he felt that civil action was more appropriate than criminal proceedings. (Social worker)

This clearly illustrates that many police officers do not have the appropriate knowledge regarding adult abuse cases. There was clear evidence from the bank that money had been taken and standing orders set up by his son without Bert's knowledge. The matter should have been referred to the Criminal Investigation Department, but Bert was deemed 'unlikely to be a good witness'. It is worrying that this attitude still persists at a time when the Home Office is trying to promote the support of vulnerable witnesses in the criminal justice system through *Action for Justice* (Home Office 1999).

Just prior to admission, Simon had contacted the police when his twin sons had started being violent but he felt they were not helpful:

> They took them out and gave them a telling off but they were back in two minutes. (Simon)

Yet there had been a positive response to reports that things were 'going missing' from Fred's house. Close circuit television cameras were put into the house to see who was going in and out. The couple next door were well known to the police. The woman was working as a prostitute in the local pubs and had recently come out of prison having served a sentence for assault.

The police had also responded quickly when neighbours had reported that they thought Howard's son had broken Howard's arm. Howard was picked up by the police on the street 'for his own protection'.

Like the social workers, police responses to allegations of elder abuse were not consistent, but erratic.

CHAPTER 5

Outcomes

At the time of finishing this book on male victims, I followed up on the current situations of the men I had interviewed, some of whom I still see on a regular basis. Eight of the men interviewed were admitted permanently to residential or nursing homes (David, Fred, Gregory, Howard, Mac, Sam, Simon and William). Gregory and Simon both suffered strokes after leaving the resource centres and currently there are concerns about both men from residential staff. Fred, Mac and Sam died very shortly after admission.

David

David is perhaps the only one who is happy and settled. His son has started to visit occasionally, the last time being when he brought his first daughter to meet her grandfather.

Gregory

Gregory's mental state deteriorated after his stroke and he now has difficulty in communicating; staff are saying that he is presenting problems because he has become very aggressive. The social worker still has concerns about the management of his finances as the situation was never resolved after placement. The carer never surrendered the bank books and no one has really taken any action until recently. Gregory is self-funding, but the home has never received any fees. The carer sold his house. It is thought that her daughter, who previously practised as a solicitor, is applying to the Court of Protection for power of attorney. The social worker is about to follow this up but had done nothing since Gregory's admission.

Simon

Simon suffered a stroke very soon after he went to live in sheltered accommodation. After discharge from hospital he went to live in residential care, but he does not like anyone to know this. His daughter told his twin sons where he was living and they now have regular contact with their father. Staff have had concerns about this; they feel the twins pressurise him into going out and they obtain money from him. In a recent review, Simon has indicated that he wants to have contact with the twins. He feels very loyal towards them. The situation is being closely monitored.

So for both Gregory and Simon, the abuses they were experiencing before admission to a place of safety have not in fact been resolved.

William

William is currently causing problems for staff in his home and for his social worker. What became clear in the follow-up discussion with the social worker was that William is still trying to come to terms with his past. The social worker was unaware of earlier life experiences which have affected William. Since being placed in care, William has become obsessional about certain things such as money matters, not having enough to eat, hoarding food, and believing his dead wife's body has been transported away by a lorry. The social worker has questioned whether he has a mental health problem. The GP said it was point-less getting an assessment of capacity because 'he would just be put on a heavy drug'. William accused his step-daughter-in-law of taking money from his bank account. The police became involved but there was no evidence of theft. The social worker visits occasionally, but no one is undertaking any in-depth work to resolve William's be-haviours.

It was suggested that William might like to attend the survivors' group; the social worker was sceptical as to the benefits William may reap but agreed to bring him to meet the group. William presented no problematic behaviours in the group meeting and said that he would like to attend regularly, which he has since done. He is able to talk about the abuse he has experienced, but work is also being un-dertaken regarding his bereavement. The social worker admits she is surprised at how well William has responded to the group work.

Howard

Howard remained in limbo for a total of 13 months. He started spending days at a local residential home to see whether he would like to live there permanently. Howard is a very passive man, and it was easy for professionals to let things drift because they know he would not complain. The concerns from the professionals have overridden Howard's choice to go home. He has now been placed permanently in a residential home which is in the same area where he has lived previously. His son, Neville, continues to live in squalor but has been given notice that he must leave the tenancy, which is in his father's name. Howard strives to be independent – he walks to the local shops every day to buy his newspaper. He still feels a sense of duty towards his son, whom he visits two to three times a week. He is taken to his previous house by taxi, which then waits five minutes while Howard goes into the house to give his son food or money.

Jim

Jim is currently waiting to move into a flat in sheltered accommodation. One of his daughters is cleaning it out and buying carpets and furniture for him. Jim has started to attend the survivors' group; he has a lot in common with Vernon and it turned out that he knew William because they used to live on the same street when they were younger.

Vernon

Vernon is living in the community and attends the survivors' group. For Vernon, the group will support him in coming to make a decision whether to stay where he is or to leave his wife. He also has a continuing need to talk about his father.

Bert

Bert attended the survivors' group, which helped him to face his imminent death and supported him when he moved into sheltered accommodation. After further case conferences, the police decided to pursue the matter of fraud by taking a statement from Bert. Sadly, Bert died peacefully shortly after moving into his flat. His sister asked the social worker if she could meet the members of the group who had supported her brother; she herself is now attending the group in order to discuss the abuse her brother experienced and to address not only her own feelings of anger, but also the loss of her brother.

Colin

Colin died recently after collapsing at home and being admitted to hospital. He stated clearly in his will that he did not want a funeral. His friends found this very difficult because they wanted to say 'good-bye' to him. Colin's wishes were respected and he was buried without any ceremony.

CHAPTER 6

Practice Issues

A critical finding of this study has been that male victims of abuse are often not offered the time and resources and sensitivity which they require, because a holistic approach has not been adopted. During adult abuse investigations, the focus is on finding out whether abuse has happened and if necessary, providing immediate safety. Good practice should involve assessing all needs, both practical and emotional, relating both to the past and the present (Pritchard 2000) and with an eye to the future. For the majority of men who participated in the project, this did not happen.

The main findings and concerns of the project are discussed below.

Inconsistency in practice

When a crisis had occurred there had consistently been a quick response from social services. However, after a place of safety had been found and the victim was placed, practices between workers differed tremendously. Some workers communicated well both with the victims and with other workers and professionals who were involved; others 'dumped' the victim and situations were left to drift for months. Practical matters such as obtaining possessions were not dealt with quickly.

Abuse procedures not followed

Even though policies and procedures were in place, very rarely were procedures followed through. Social workers regularly failed to

- conduct a formal interview with the victim

- ask the victim if he wanted the police involved

- liaise with other professionals who could have information (e.g. probation officers)

- convene a case conference

- develop a formal protection plan

- reconvene the case conference to review the protection plan.

Allegations and judgements

When there was uncertainty about the victim's mental state, allegations were sometimes not taken seriously and not followed through. The police regularly refused to come out to interview victims, who were deemed not to be good witnesses. Where there is uncertainty about a victim's mental state, then expert assessment should be organised as quickly as possible.

Assessments

Again because of other pressures, not enough time was spent assessing the needs of victims. Basic assessments when carried out were often rushed; little preparation was put into obtaining background information (as in the case of Gregory) and assessing need in relation to past and present problems. The tendency was to deal with the presenting problem and not to pursue needs resulting from the effects of the abuse. There was little evidence that all the unresolved practical and emotional issues were identified or realistic plans made for their adequate resolution in the short and long term.

Lack of time

If the new way of working under the care management system is not allowing workers the time to assess properly, surely that system is abusing the victim even more? If social workers have not got the time to work with someone, then it is necessary to look elsewhere to find people who can support and help a victim in the long term. For victims from different countries, it is very important to find someone who can help them to communicate in their own language. Being abused is frightening enough, but to be left thinking about everything inside your own mind, and not being able to discuss it with anyone in your own language, is yet another abuse. Victims who are confused could experience the same sense of isolation if people with skills in communication are not brought in to work with them.

Lack of communication

No Secrets stresses the importance of working on an inter-agency basis (Department of Health 2000a). Good communication is needed to achieve this. However, communication within agencies also needs to be improved. Residential staff in particular need information about the victim, his background, and the circumstances surrounding admission to care. Following admission, both the victim and relevant workers need to be informed about the progress of the adult abuse investigation. Updating the key individuals is fundamental to good practice.

Principles ignored

This study found that values stated in the National Health Service and Community Care Act 1990 and the basic principles of adult abuse work were either ignored or seriously misrepresented – namely self-determination, choice and equal opportunities. Frequently actions were taken against the wishes of the victim, the most disturbing example being William, who was adamant that he did not want to go into residential care; he and care staff who supported him were overridden. Howard desperately wanted to go home but, having remained in the resource centre for 13 months, he was placed in residential care. On the other hand, there is evidence, especially preceding admission to a place of safety, that self-determination and choice are sometimes cynically used to justify the inaction of workers.

Choice was limited. Once a decision had been made about permanent care, the victim was placed quickly – in some cases not having been shown the home at all. This was misleading for some victims, who thought that a residential home would be similar to a resource centre.

CHAPTER 7

Conclusion

It is now readily accepted that male children may suffer abuse in their own homes and from adults who are assumed to be caring for them. This project confirms and illustrates the less frequently known fact that adult males – particularly those in old age – may also be victims in a range of abusive situations not dissimilar from those experienced by older women.

The quantitative study which was carried out in the three social services departments found a substantial number of male victims. Because of their adherence to social expectations, it is likely that many men do not disclose the abuse they suffer; therefore, the real prevalence is likely to be much higher than is acknowledged either by victims or by the services. To date, research into this aspect of abuse has been limited but the findings of this project would indicate a need for further research regarding prevalence and incidence. If the public and the professionals are not aware of the extent of this problem, male victims are likely to remain well hidden and not to receive the help and services they require to leave the abusive situation or to deal with their feelings about it – feelings which are frequently ambivalent or confused.

There is a clear need to move away from social stereo-typing in which the typical victim is female and the typical abuser is male. This project has shown that the abuse of males should be defined in a wider context and not solely in terms of the previous definitions of abuse commonly used in child abuse and domestic violence work. Thus, for example, financial abuse was the most common form of abuse experienced by men in both the quantitative and qualitative studies within the project.

As men grow older they frequently become more vul-nerable and at greater risk of abuse from both male and female perpetrators. It is sometimes argued that physical and mental ageing may cause undue stress among carers of older people, and that this stress leads to abusive outbursts. An earlier study (Pritchard 2000) has challenged this sim-plistic causal belief in respect of the abuse of older women, and the present study found that carer's stress was not a causal factor in the abuse of the men. This supports the argument that elder abuse is often a very complex issue, which necessitates professional understanding of past life experiences and relationships and their links to present problems. Workers need time to undertake in-depth work both with victims and abusers not only during initial inves-tigations but also in the longer term work. It was evident in the study that such methods of working are not regularly adopted. Pressures on workers are such that they tend to make quick rough-and-ready assessments and rarely undertake long-term therapeutic work to ensure the achievement of outcomes which match victims' physical and emotional needs.

Workers in all settings need to be aware that some men can experience different forms of abuse through their lifetime. As with female victims, they can go through life having developed strategies to cope, but in later adulthood there may be earlier unresolved issues which need attention and resolution. The project identified the following needs:

- to talk about abuse (past and recent), life experiences, dilemmas and fears for the future, the resolution of loyalties which have been abused

- to be given practical information and advice about sources of help

- to be offered options about possible actions and outcomes

- to go at the victim's pace, respecting the stresses involved in disclosing one's failure to cope effectively with those who have abused, and with one's fears of future suffering and disappointment.

Professor Robert Pinker (1978) defined a social services client as a person who receives what the social services call help and who lives with the consequences of that help. This study has shown twelve older men receiving and living with 'help'. The professional and administrative task is to ensure that referral to social services does not constitute a double whammy of abuse. Especially the kind of abuse arising from the perversion of professional values like 'self-determination' in ways which justify the idleness and indifference of professional workers.

Few of the men interviewed received a good service. Many of them were 'dumped' in a place of safety; little work was done in relation to how they felt about the abuse they had experienced or regarding their fears for the future. As with any victim (child or adult), there needs to be reassurance that it is all right and safe to talk about abuse and that one will be respected and believed. The study found that few workers felt confident in this area of work and avoided discussing such topics. This would indicate a need for more effective selection of specialist staff and for training in developing skills in how to communicate honestly with a victim, how to deal with mixed and confused feelings, and how to work with a victim in the longer term. Social workers frequently put forward the argument that they have not got time to do long-term work; they also admitted that they do not have the knowledge and skills to undertake this specialised area of work. Consequently the men were often left to deal with their own feelings while the workers dealt only with the practical issues.

The men who are currently attending the survivors' group welcome the opportunity to talk about their past lives, the abuses and their feelings. It seems that although some people continue to stereotype men as wanting to keep things to themselves, the reality is that men do have a need to talk, to come to terms with what has happened to them and to find emotional healing. The healing process is just as important to male victims as it is to women, and should be made a moral as well as a professional priority.

To sum up: the project has found that men who are abused and take the important step of disclosing the fact may not receive the help and support they require. It is a sad comment that we still tend to think in terms of children and women as the main victims of abuse, and have not addressed the problem of male victims – a problem which is probably much more widespread than we dare to think. It is a social policy issue which must be addressed in the future.

References

Appleby, G.A. and Anastas, J.W. (1998) 'Violence in the lives of lesbians and gay men.' In their *Not Just a Passing Phase: Social Work with Gay, Lesbian and Bisexual People.* New York: Columbia University Press.

Baker, A. A. (1975) 'Granny battering.' *Modern Geriatrics 5*, 8, 20–24.

Biggs, S., Phillipson, C. and Kingston, P. (1995) *Elder Abuse in Perspective.* Buckingham: Open University Press.

Burston, G.R. (1975) 'Granny battering.' *British Medical Journal 3*, September, 592–593.

Burston, G.R. (1977) 'Do your elderly patients live in fear of being battered?' *Modern Geriatrics 7*, 5, 54–55.

Clough, R. (1988) 'Scandals in residential care: a report to the Wagner Committee.' Unpublished.

Department of Health (1992) *Confronting Elder Abuse.* London: HMSO.

Department of Health (1993) *No Longer Afraid: The Safeguard of Older People in Domestic Settings.* London: HMSO.

Department of Health (2000a) *No Secrets: Guidance on Developing and Implementing Multi-Agency Policies and Procedures to Protect Vulnerable Adults from Abuse.* London: HMSO.

Department of Health (2000b) *'No Secrets': Guidance on Developing Multi-Agency Policies and Procedures to Protect Vulnerable Adults from Abuse.* Health Service/Local Authority Circular HSC 2000/007. London: NHS Executive.

Eastman, M. (1984) *Old Age Abuse.* London: Age Concern.

Etherington, K. (1995) *Adult Male Survivors of Childhood Sexual Abuse.* Brighton: Pavilion Publishing.

Farley, N. (1992) 'Same-sex domestic violence.' In S. Dworkin and F. Guitterez (eds) *Counseling Gay Men and Lesbians: Journey to the End of the Rainbow.* Alexandria, VA: ACA.

Gelles, R.J. (1997) *Intimate Violence,* 3rd ed. Thousand Oaks, CA: Sage.

Gelles, R.J. and Cornell, C.P. (1985) *Intimate Violence in Families.* Beverly Hills, CA: Sage.

Gelles, R.J. and Straus, M.A. (1988) *Intimate Violence.* New York: Simon and Schuster.

Home Office (1996) *Domestic Violence.* Home Office Research Study 191. London: HMSO.

Home Office (1999) *Action for Justice.* London: HMSO.

Hunter, M. (1990) *Abused Boys: The Neglected Victims of Sexual Abuse.* New York: Ballantine.

Island, D. and Letellier, P. (1991) *Men Who Beat the Men Who Love Them.* Binghamton, NY: Harrington Park Press.

Kent Social Services Department (1987) *Practice Guidelines for Dealing with Elder Abuse.* Maidstone: Kent County Council.

Landolt, M.A. and Dutton, D.G. (1997) 'Power and personality: an analysis of gay male intimate abuse.' *Sex Roles 37,* 5/6, 335–359.

Lord Chancellor's Department. (1997) *Who Decides? Making Decisions on Behalf of Mentally Incapacitated Adults.* London: The Stationery Office.

McCreadie, C. (1996) *Elder Abuse: Update on Research.* London: Institute of Gerontology, King's College.

Mendel, M. (1995) *The Male Survivor: The Impact of Sexual Abuse.* Thousand Oaks, CA: Sage.

Pinker, R. (1978) *Social Work and Social Policy: Identities and Purposes.* London: Chelsea College, University of London.

Pritchard, J. (1993) 'Gang warfare.' *Community Care,* 8 July, 22–23.

Pritchard, J. (1995) *The Abuse of Older People,* 2nd ed. London: Jessica Kingsley Publishers.

Pritchard, J. (2000) *The Needs of Older Women: Services for Victims of Elder Abuse and Other Abuse.* Bristol: Policy Press.

Riley, P. (1989) 'Professional dilemmas in elder abuse.' Unpublished.

Steinmetz, S.K. (1978) 'The battered husband syndrome.' *Victimology 2,* 499–509.

Straus, M. (1999) 'The controversy over domestic violence by women.' In X.B. Arriaga and S. Oskamp (eds) *Violence in Intimate Relationships.* Thousand Oaks, CA: Sage.

Straus, M.A. and Gelles, R.J. (1986) 'Societal change and change in family violence from 1975 to 1985 as revealed by two national surveys.' *Journal of Marriage and the Family 48,* 465–479.

Straus, M.A., Gelles, R.J. and Steinmetz, S.K. (1980) *Behind Closed Doors: Violence in the American Family.* Garden City, NY: Anchor.

Tomlin, S. (1989) *Abuse of Elderly People: An Unnecessary and Preventable Problem.* London: British Geriatrics Society.

Wagner Committee (1988) *Residential Care: A Positive Choice.* London: HMSO.

Subject Index

Author Index